PROVEN MARKETING STRATEGIES FOR COACHES AND CONSULTANTS TO ATTRACT YOUR DREAM CLIENTS

by Chris Gold

CONTENTS

Proven Marketing Strategies for coaches and consultants To Attract Your Dream Clients

There are just 5 ways to increase your revenue and your profits	1
1. Lead Gen with Facebook Advertising	2
2. Increase Website Conversion with Visual Website Optimizer	3
3. Increase the amount of purchases from existing customers using Loyalty Schemes	4
4. Increase average spend by using Google Remarketing	5
5. Increase your margins by Removing the Bad Apples	6
Marketing Strategies Proven To Deliver Dream Clients	7
Why You Should Attract Dream Clients?	8
What Is Marketing?	10
Here's My Dream For You	11
The Most Important Thing To Do	12
1. Facebook Advertising	13
How To Get Free Consults With Facebook Ads?	14
2. Strategic Product Selling	18
3. Webinars	21
4. Diversification	22

Which One Should You Do First?	23
The Benefits of These Marketing Strategies	24
Why Free Consultations Work?	28
Improving Your Marketing Campaigns with Landing Pages	31
Landing Pages 101	32
Powering your marketing campaigns with landing pages	36
What kind of traffic to send to your landing pages	40
Start with strong, contextual images	44
Your Headline and Sub-headline	46
Add your call to action	48
Sharing the (most important) benefits of your offer	49
Brag a bit: a dash of social proof	50
Keep improving by running an A/B test	53
Moving forward: ideas for action	55
Get in the Driver's Seat	57

THERE ARE JUST 5 WAYS TO INCREASE YOUR REVENUE AND YOUR PROFITS

1. Increase leads
2. Increase conversion
3. Increase amount purchased
4. Increase average spend
5. Increase margin

If you can increase all of these levers then you can massively increase your profits.

Example:

If your revenue is 100,000 and your profit is 10,000 then you would only need to increase each of the 5 levers by 1% and you would increase your profits by 50%.

In this example if you can increase each lever by 2% then you will double your profits.

So let's look at each area:

1. LEAD GEN WITH FACEBOOK ADVERTISING

Although I now generate leads via lots of different channels my current favourite is Facebook Advertising because it's so cheap right now, it's very targeted and I actually don't know anyone who is not on Facebook so I can potentially advertise to any group of people in the western world.

Top Tip 1: When creating an ad you can narrow down by selecting what you think your audience is interested in. Think about what all of your customers like: What books they read, what magazines they read and what tools they use. Then choose these in 'interests" and you will be targeting other prospects who are similar to your customers.

Top Tip 2: You can also upload email addresses or telephone numbers from your database into Facebook. Then Facebook will quickly cross check to see if they have a Facebook account & if they do you can create Custom Audiences & either advertise just to these or create a "Similar Audience". This is very powerful and very targeted and a great way to re-generate old leads into new customers.

Top Tip 3: Like my page here to find out more about Facebook marketing

2. INCREASE WEBSITE CONVERSION WITH VISUAL WEBSITE OPTIMIZER

Although I use several website optimization tools my favourite is Visual Website Optimizer.

Visual Website Optimizer

It allows me to split test different aspects of my website pages. So for example, I can test a green 'buy button" versus a red 'buy button" to see which one performs the best.

Top Tip 1: Google Analytics also allows you to split test.

Top Tip 2: Before you start spending money on Optimization tools make sure you have a decent amount of traffic. 1000 Visitors per month.

3. INCREASE THE AMOUNT OF PURCHASES FROM EXISTING CUSTOMERS USING LOYALTY SCHEMES

Introducing loyalty schemes into your business, where you reward customers who buy more can range from giving them prize points or giving them cash back.

Top Tip 1: Try and think out of the box here. Although people like gifts they also like experiences so if you can provide your top customers with entertainment whether that be a wine tasting event, a day at the races or a free place at one of your seminars this will work like a charm and will also give you the opportunity to bond and get to know them better.

Top Tip 2: Another good way to increase purchases is to introduce: "Customers who bought this product also bought these" at the checkout stage. How many times have you been swayed on Amazon because of this tactic?

4. INCREASE AVERAGE SPEND BY USING GOOGLE REMARKETING

Ever feel like you have been followed round the web by the same advert?

This is "Google Remarketing" and it's very simple to implement. By adding some code provided by Google to your site each visitor will be tagged & if they didn't enter your sales funnel then you can create an advert that is only shown to these visitors on Google's massive display network (Basically millions of websites including YouTube that display Google's adverts)

Top Tip: If you want to increase your customers average spend then if you have multiple products, you can just target customers who have already purchased from you as they are much more likely to buy more.

5. INCREASE YOUR MARGINS BY REMOVING THE BAD APPLES

You can obviously increase your margins by negotiating better prices with your suppliers and/or increasing your prices.

Top Tip: Pareto's 80:20 Law will suggest that 20% of your customers will bring in 80% of your revenue and usually the bottom 10% of your customers will lose you money and take up most of your time. By increasing your prices you will usually lose these bottom 10% anyway but if you don't then it's time to weed them out and get rid of them.

Top Tip 2: The above is also usually true of your products if you have a product line. So get rid of those underperforming products and consolidate your efforts into those that perform.

Bonus Tip: If your margin is 30% and you increase your prices by 10% you can afford to lose 25% of your customers. Conversely if you reduce your prices by 10% you would need to find 50% more customers - usually the 'price conscious moaning" ones as well!

I use little-practiced marketing strategies to attract my dream clients for years now. These clients are high-paying and they can make your business a success. But first, it is important to know what marketing is. It is also essential to know how to create a powerful marketing strategy. Today, I am going to reveal the marketing strategies I used so you can start implementing them into your business.

MARKETING STRATEGIES PROVEN TO DELIVER DREAM CLIENTS

WHY YOU SHOULD ATTRACT DREAM CLIENTS?

One of the things I've discovered on this journey is even if coaching and speaking are great, if I can't attract my dream clients I'd be trapped.

In that scenario, I would just keep holding onto my dream of being a speaker but remain unable to reach it. When you have a marketing strategy that draws in massive amounts of people to see you and connect with you and consume your products, more dreams become possible.

This begs the question: Who are the dream clients? These are your high-end clients. They are the ones you love working and spending time with. At the same time, they want to be around you. It's exciting and exhilarating to help them.

A dream client is also somebody whose dreams you help make come true. They may be coming to you for financial advice. They may have a dream of retiring one day and traveling to holiday destinations. You're helping them realize those dreams.

You may have clients who come in and their dream is to heal themselves or be in the best shape of their lives. You may have clients whom you teach relationships to, so they can find their dream spouse.

It doesn't matter what field you're in. One of the goals is to help our clients' dreams come true.

Dream clients also pay you what you're worth. In the process, you can run a dream business anywhere in the world and enjoy your dream lifestyle.

If you think about a marketing strategy to acquire dream clients, you're giving yourself the opportunity to have your dream lifestyle. Your dream lifestyle will give you the freedom of money and time. With this freedom, you can have more chances to go after more dreams. It's a pretty good game. You and the clients both win.

WHAT IS MARKETING?

Marketing is a platform, strategy or vehicle to help your dreams come true. Many people say, "Marketing is so confusing" or "Where do I even begin?" The great thing about a marketing strategy is you can learn it like a game and have fun with it.

I told myself, "It's too painful to chase after clients, try to get booked on stages all the time, and be in the hustle of marketing." You know what I'm saying? The hustle is chasing people.

The opposite of the hustle is dream clients coming to you. It doesn't mean you don't work hard or put an effort into building a tactical marketing plan or system but when you start building it, people are and will be coming to you.

Chasing clients is no fun. I did it for years. In the sales business, we had to go after clients and network.

Then I did it in this business. I had to go get on stages and chase people at networking events. I had to get on the phone and call people. Now, I pick up the phone and call people about dreams and ideas I have. My clients come to me with an intelligent marketing strategy and a marketing mix.

HERE'S MY DREAM FOR YOU

My dream is to teach you some marketing strategies to make you say, "Wow, this is starting to make sense" or "Wow, I can see myself doing this." Then, if it makes sense and you can see yourself doing it, the key is for you to do it.

I don't expect you to become a master marketer in only one or two sessions. What I want you to do is to stick to a particular marketing strategy and to continue to learn and try things.

I'm going to give you some proven strategies. I can share with you is there's no one right way to slice bread. I'm going to give you multiple options today and I want you to understand why these things work. Most importantly, by the end of this article, you will understand marketing.

THE MOST IMPORTANT THING TO DO

I have four marketing strategies and I'll begin with the simplest ones. Our goal is to get clients into a free consultation.

You think about marketing today and say, "Oh, I'm marketing so I can sell my products. I can just sell my products, make lots of money from my products and get my message out there. I don't have to do sales calls anymore."

I'm going to give you a different approach to this and provide you with methods so you can achieve it. Now, a free consultation is about 45 minutes. During that time, you coach people and make an offer. From the free consultation, our goal is to get people to experience what we can do and then get them into a high-end program.
What makes our online marketing fun, super profitable, and great at bringing dream clients in? Getting them on the phone. What are the different marketing strategies to help you get a free consultation with dream clients?

Let's begin.

1. FACEBOOK ADVERTISING

One of the most basic marketing strategies is running Facebook ads through social media. Social media marketing is a good strategy, to begin with. We're actually teaching our clients to set up and manage these ads to get free consultations.

One of the biggest concerns people have about online marketing is how they can drive traffic. A lot of people will talk about strategic partners which I think is a great way to grow a business. I do product launches with strategic partners which promote me.

One of my goals after doing the product launches on social media which brought us seven figures was to try to create a system that brings in dream clients to our business every single day.

I have been running social media ads, particularly Facebook ads for years but about a year and a half ago, I thought, "What would it be like to take that one launch and do it every single month?"

We're not doing seven figures every single month in our business with this strategy but we did about $350,000 in sales on average by running Facebook ads. I want to teach you how we achieve that.

I can't guarantee your results, as they can vary significantly. However, if I were you, I would be stepping in to learn this stuff so I could do it for my business.

HOW TO GET FREE CONSULTS WITH FACEBOOK ADS?

There are different marketing strategies to offer a free consultation with Facebook ads:

1. Use a Video To Offer A Free Gift
Let people watch a video which offers a free consultation. Many people on social media love to watch videos.

The best thing about this strategy is you give your high-end clients something they can consume before they get on with the free consultation. That way, they get to know you and your brand.

2. Give Them Awesome Content
A good content marketing strategy is essential for any business. I talked about the importance of great content marketing in one of my live-streams. I said content starts to add value and gives people an idea of the value they would receive if and when they build a coaching relationship with you. It's important they understand who you are and what you do. How can you help them?

If I'm watching this video and I'm a client, I would think, "How can David help me?" As I watch David's video, I get my answer. He's teaching me three things which can help me. Now I'm getting value from him. I know who he is.

All throughout the video, he's telling people, "Hey, if you really like this, I want to encourage you to go book a free Man on Fire consultation. During the consultation, I can help you do this, this, and this." Throughout the video, he's making calls to action for them to go book a free consultation. Make sense? He's giving a free consultation to sell $5,000 programs through a video.

3. Let Them Know When Something Is Coming
If you just go, "Hey, go book this free consultation" directly, you'll probably get fewer people. You may also have an unqualified person on the phone.

I would suggest not having the call-to-action button pop up on the video until half the running time. You can also say, "Hey, in a few minutes, the button's going to pop up for you to book a free consultation if you want to have a Man on Fire free consultation with me."

They know it's coming but they have to wait, consume the information, and have some resonance with you.

By doing this, you don't need to spend your entire time during the consultation convincing them why you're an expert. In the video, you're teaching, telling your story, and sharing testimonials from your clients. You've already established yourself as an expert. You become an instant authority online. Instantly, you have credibility which people all over the world can see. It's a game changer.

When you think about this, it's one of the simplest marketing strategies you can set up and run. The key is to give more quality content, so your dream clients can also have a quality conversation with you.

Now, they could consume a whole bunch of content but then get on the phone and it turns out they're broke. Expect that. You're going to have a bunch of conversations with potential people who don't have money but you're going to find a conversation where you can truly attract the person to invest in your coaching program

4. Fill Out A Questionnaire

One of my marketing strategies for Facebook ads and video is to let these clients fill out a questionnaire.

The way David has done it in his business is he will actually have them fill out a questionnaire before they get on. Then, he can look through the questionnaire. If they're not a good fit, he sends them an email and tells them they didn't qualify. He gets to weed out the people who don't look committed. After all, in his questionnaire, he gets to ask, "On a scale of 1 to 10, how committed are you to doing this?"

If you look at the questionnaire and you say, "I don't want to get on the phone with them," then you just chuck it. You only get on the phone with people who look good. Make sense?

How do you get them to fill out a questionnaire? You can say, "Hey, I'm going to give you an opportunity to get a free consultation. Fill out the questionnaire below. You'll submit it to me and if you qualify to get a free consultation with us based on your response, we'll let you know."

One of the biggest mistakes in marketing strategies is to keep thinking, "Free is free is free is free." When you do free all the way, you can't get high-end clients. When you put barriers to entry in your marketing like filling out a questionnaire to qualify people, it can be just as good as the money put down to get on the phone.

5. Let Them Make A Down Payment

In fact, you can make them watch a certain amount of the video, let them fill out the questionnaire, and you say, "Hey, to get on the phone for a free consultation, you have to put down a deposit today of $97 that's fully refundable."

I don't think you need to do it out of the gate. As you start getting a ton of free consultations, you can put the $97 deposit down as a barrier to entry. That way, you're getting even more quality people.

2. STRATEGIC PRODUCT SELLING

Another of our marketing strategies is product selling but this is going to be unique. Once they download the free gift through a Facebook ad video, they see a page making an offer on a product.

We call these our entry-level products since they are priced $37 or $97. This how these products work: If they buy a product from us, we will get them into a free consultation. From the free consult, we offer an opportunity for them to become a dream client.

To be more specific, once they buy a product from us, then we send them a video offering a free consultation. Either way, in both marketing strategies, your clients get a free consultation. The difference here is they've purchased a product and now they're a customer.

Making An Impact

Why do we do this? One, again, this technique acts as a barrier entry, weeding out less-qualified people. Second, it shows the client's commitment to your program.

Let me say this: Of course, our goal here is to get people to buy products. Working one-on-one with dream clients is not my only goal. When people buy our products, it gets our tools and our coaching into the hands of as many people as possible. This way, I can truly make an impact with our story. I can help empower them to become coaches and speakers, go out, and make a difference in the world.

I like this because we get to impact way more people. If somebody comes to a free consult and they never become a client, we're still impacting them. They're still taking steps and consuming the step-by-step systems to help them to get clients, results, and impact.

Repeat Customers

What I've discovered while doing these marketing strategies is when somebody becomes a customer, they're more likely to buy again. I like getting buyers because they tend to make additional buying decisions.

In a video, you can say, "Hey, congratulations. Because you're a customer, we want to offer you a free dream clients delivery coaching session." This video offers them the free consult, they show up to the free consult, and we coach and help them clear their vision. We talk to them about the challenges preventing them from getting their dream clients and give them a plan and path to go out and start getting clients in the next 30 days to 60 days.

Our free consult is valuable. If they decide to work with us and join one of our higher-tier programs, then awesome. Of course, it's our goal, because we know if people work with us in our higher-tier programs, they're going to get to their dreams and visions faster. If they don't, then we've added a tremendous amount of value to our customers, and they're going to remember us for it.

We'll sell programs as high as $40,000 on the phone to clients through this system. We have others here too who sell below or above such number. We give options for people when they come to this free consult, so they can start where they want and make a bigger decision. This is one we've been running for a while and we've been running it super successfully.

3. WEBINARS

Another of the marketing strategies that work is a webinar. It's different from social media or Facebook ads where they can watch 10 minutes of me on video or one of my clients offering the free consult. The effect is instant.

With the webinar, they actually have to sign up to gain access, so there's an immediate barrier to entry. They sign up for the webinar and show up. My webinar's an hour long but here's the thing. Unless they're on the webinar for 45 minutes, they cannot book a free consultation.

Why do I do this? If I'm going to give them a free consult and use my team's resources, they need to show me they're willing to show up, invest 45+ minutes watching a webinar, and invest another 45 minutes on a phone call before we will let them into our community.

This works because we're making them consume the information and we're putting up these barriers. By the time they get there, they know what my system's about.

When they get on the phone with the coach, they know what they're looking for. I've told them the path. I've shared the steps to being successful. Now, if they want it, they get to join the program.

4. DIVERSIFICATION

All these marketing strategies work for us. Still, people ask, "Why do all these instead of just one?" I'll give you another strategy which works for us too. It's called diversification.

What happened if something happens and my ultimate marketing plan doesn't work and stops producing results? I like to have multiple marketing strategies to bring in dream clients. I know if one thing is doing better than the other at any given time, I'm strong here.

WHICH ONE SHOULD YOU DO FIRST?

When you have multiple marketing strategies and limited resources, the challenge is determining which one you should do first. If I were you, I would choose the fastest path.

Usually, I use a Facebook ad for a video. If you're not comfortable doing a video, as you probably don't want to be seen, make a webinar with a PowerPoint and your voice. You can do 10 minutes of just slides with very valuable content.

You can also go a much longer route which is just as effective. For example, you can have a webinar presentation which is 45 minutes to an hour long. It takes a little bit more mastery to do it but it works great. Choose the path you want.

If you're still confused, get a free consult with one of our coaches and consider your options of how we could serve you more deeply with this.

THE BENEFITS OF THESE MARKETING STRATEGIES

You need to understand marketing and answer the most basic questions like "Why does this work?" or "In the grand scheme of things, why does this make sense for building a really intelligent business?" The reality is a couple things.

1. They Help Control The Game

When you're running Facebook ads or employing the other marketing strategies, you control the game. You are not dependent on a strategic partner for your promotion and product launches. You're not dependent upon getting booked on a stage.

With these marketing strategies, you can start really small and you can grow your own marketing.

2. They Grow Your Marketing List

These marketing strategies deliver dream clients for free consultations but that's not all. They help you build a list.

An email list gives you longer-term success. You can build a growing community of buyers. Having a lot of buyers who are consuming your stuff and talking to you is an asset.

The cool thing is that an email list can work on repeat. Today, your list will get an email saying, "Hey, go book a free consultation with us." Days later or even a year after, they'll get pretty much the same thing.

This is important because you never know when they're going to respond. Doing this on repeat gives your list a chance to make a big investment decision anytime.

A lot of times people go, "I need to make money right now. I need to be profitable." An email list can give you that. Since it's a long-term marketing plan, you'll make even more money, have even more people, have a system set up, and be able to build for the future.

Because you have a list of your dream clients, you have options for your marketing strategies.

For example, you can now look for a strategic partnership. It's harder to do it when you don't have an asset or a system. When you have a system to bringing in leads every single day, you become valuable in the marketplace.

3. They Let You Choose Your Clients

It's not enough to simply know these marketing strategies or even master them. You have to determine why you're getting in the game of doing this. For me, it's when I have a system, I don't have to chase clients ever again. It's freedom!

There's also freedom of being able to choose your dream clients. One day, I was on the phone with one of my salespeople who had a client who was indecisive. My salesperson said, "We just need to cut this person loose because we want to work with dream clients who are ready to get into action and do this thing."

The freedom of choosing your client and never having to chase one is not only wonderful but also liberating.

4. They Allow You To Dictate The Price

A lot of times people look at my stuff and ask, "How are you charging what you're charging?" The reality to me is I think our programs are really reasonable.

We've created all these different tiers so they're reasonable — period. There are many tiers people can get in on. Everything we do is reasonable. There's a ladder the clients can climb.

The main reason I can command the type of pricing I do is I know this stuff and have developed skill sets which make me good at a lot of different things.

If you can control your marketing, it means you control pricing too. You're not in this place of desperation to take on clients who are below your standard.

It doesn't mean they all need to have the same dreams but they should have dreams and aspirations. Why would you want to spend any personal time with people who don't have aspirations and dreams? You wouldn't. You would want them to go through your digital programs and build themselves up so they can create dreams and see for themselves it's possible for them to have what they want. Then they can be in proximity or in the same space as you. Make sense?

5. They Create Systems That Work

Doing these marketing strategies is liberation. It's freedom. You've got a choice. You can go, "I'm going to go for traditional models and speak on stages and network."

There's nothing wrong with that. To me, it's like the icing on the cake. I still go to events and I network. I still go speak on stages but it's not a necessity.

What is necessary is creating marketing strategies and systems which will work. It's understanding this stuff and learning to play the game.

WHY FREE CONSULTATIONS WORK?

Why does the free consult work? It does because you've created a structure allowing people to funnel into your world. They come into your world and they start consuming your content.

It doesn't matter whether it's a 10-minute long video and it sends them over a free consult. It doesn't matter whether they buy our product first, then watch a video, and then they go to a free consult.

They come in and they're consuming content. They're getting familiar with you and they understand how you can help them.

Every step of the way, not only are they consuming but there is also a barrier here which prevents the wrong people from getting in on the free consult. In my webinar, I can let them put down $500 to get on the phone.

The barrier is their time and commitment to show up.

Even on the webinar, I sell them on doing it and talk them out of it if they're not the right fit. I'll tell them, "If you're not ready to invest your time, your energy, and your money into your business, don't get on the free consultation. Don't do it."

When people buy, the dynamics change. They've already invested their money, and they're already my clients, so I encourage them to get on.

This is an added value for people who are already my clients. My thinking is that I want to spend the time with them since they invested money in us. They invested time in our community. We want to be on the phone with you because you've already made the commitment.

Weeding out people who haven't made the commitment doesn't mean they're not qualified. They just might not have bought an online product yet.

In fact, they actually know what they want but perhaps they're not looking for the lower-tier stuff. They know they want to go straight there.

IMPROVING YOUR MARKETING CAMPAIGNS WITH LANDING PAGES

LANDING PAGES 101

Never start a marketing campaign without a dedicated landing page.

Ever.

But what exactly *is* a landing page? How is it different from your homepage or another page on your website and how will Unbounce help you build 'em?

So. many. questions.

But, hey, that's why you're here.

By the time you complete this three part ecourse, you'll learn why you should be using landing pages to power all of your marketing campaigns, what makes an especially persuasive landing page, and how to build your landing pages.

Asa marketer you need to improve your campaign results and do more with less. You know deliver more leads on the same budget.

So this is the classic marketing problem. Do you focus on getting more traffic or do you focus on converting the visitors you already have?

You focus on conversion!

That way your campaigns aren't just seen by more people but they are also more effective.

This is exactly what dedicated landing pages can do for you. They are the best way to increase your conversion rates.

Landing pages will power your most effective campaigns.

What is a landing page?

Technically, a landing page is any webpage that someone lands on after clicking an online marketing call-to-action. But we need a more focused definition here.

As a marketer, it's important for you to get the best bang for your buck and ensure that as much traffic hitting your landing pages *actually* converts. So for our purposes, we're going to define a landing page as a dedicated, campaign-specific webpage that drives your visitors to complete a single marketing goal or call to action.

A landing page is a dedicated, campaign-specific webpage that drives visitors to complete a single marketing goal or call to action.

By **dedicated**, we mean that the page has (virtually) no ties to your website, and serves only one purpose: getting your visitors to convert through a single call to action.

By **campaign-specific**, we mean that for each initiative or marketing campaign you run, you should have a tailored page *just* for that campaign. One ebook? One landing page. Two promotions? Two landing pages.

If you compare your homepage to a landing page, you'll see why landing pages are so important to the success of your campaigns.

Your homepage is designed with a more general purpose in mind. It's your Brand Central Station. It speaks to your overall brand and corporate values and is typically loaded with links and navigation to other areas of your site. It's designed to encourage explor-

ation.
- Designed for many purposes
- Contains many links and navigation points
- Encourages exploration rather than conversion

Your dedicated landing pages are designed for one purpose only: Conversions!

Think of the links on your pages as leaks. Each link on a page that doesn't support your conversion goal (e.g. ebook downloads) is a distraction that will dilute your message and reduce your conversion rate.

The ratio of links on a landing page to the number of campaign conversion goals is called Attention Ratio. In an optimized campaign, your attention ratio should be 1:1. Because every campaign has one goal, every corresponding landing page should have only one call to action – one place to click.

Landing pages produce better campaign results because – by dedicating themselves to just one action with an attention ratio of 1:1 – they narrow a visitor's focus and get more people to follow through with your call to action.

As an example, let's say you wanted to give away an ebook as part of a lead generation campaign. To get the highest conversion rates and encourage the most downloads, you'd send that campaign's traffic to a dedicated landing page instead of your homepage or another page on your website. You'd link to this landing page anytime you wanted to promote downloads and collect leads.

1. Page is dedicated to one purpose with no navigation to your website
2. Page is campaign specific with just a single campaign goal
3. Contains only one call to action

Question: How many calls to action should a landing page include?

Answer: Only one! Landing pages aren't designed to function as a microsite or any info-heavy addition to your website. A good landing page only includes the info needed to prompt a campaign-relation action from your target audience.

POWERING YOUR MARKETING CAMPAIGNS WITH LANDING PAGES

In the context of your larger marketing campaigns, landing pages serve one of two purposes.

1. To capture leads that enable you to market to people in the future, or
2. To "warm up" potential customers to the product you are trying to sell to them before sending them further into your sales funnel.

In other words, you'll either use **a lead generation page** or **a click-through page**, depending on your campaign's goal.

Here's a lead gen page from a fictional real estate agency, Emerald Developments. Note that all the copy on the page appeals to a home seller's top concerns and supports a single campaign goal. When visitors fill out the form — the only call to action on the page — they're exchanging their contact info for a complimentary home valuation & offer estimate.

Because the landing page has an attention ratio of 1:1, focusing on just one goal (versus a regular page on a website which would contain links to a variety of other pages), visitors are far more likely to complete the intended call-to-action without getting distracted.

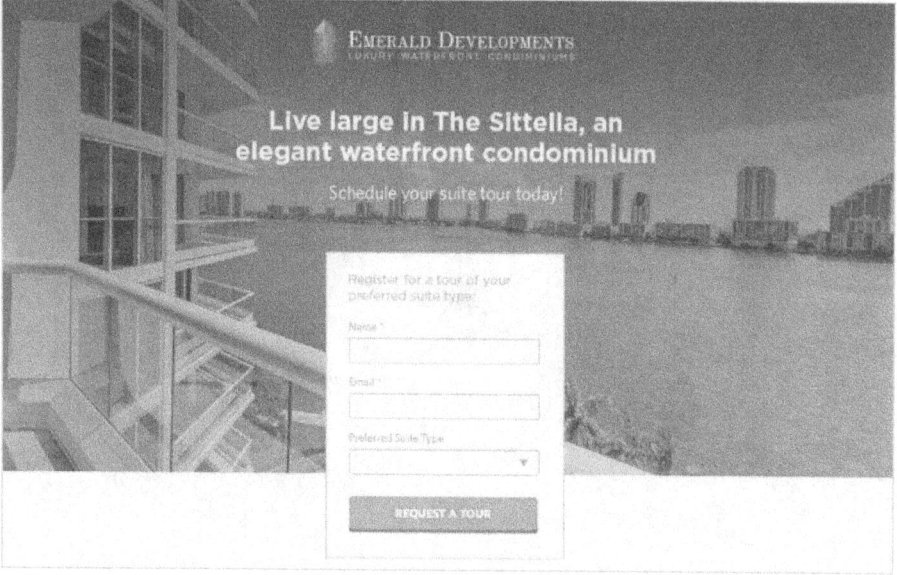

A click-through page is used to push visitors further into a funnel — usually for e-commerce purchases.

These pages exist to persuade someone of your product or service's value. Click-through pages drive leads further into your marketing funnel and the call to action button usually directs visitors to a free trial, demo, shopping cart, pricing page, or checkout.

Here's an example of an Emerald Developments click-through where the intent is to share the value proposition, and drive visitors to click through to the next stage in the funnel.

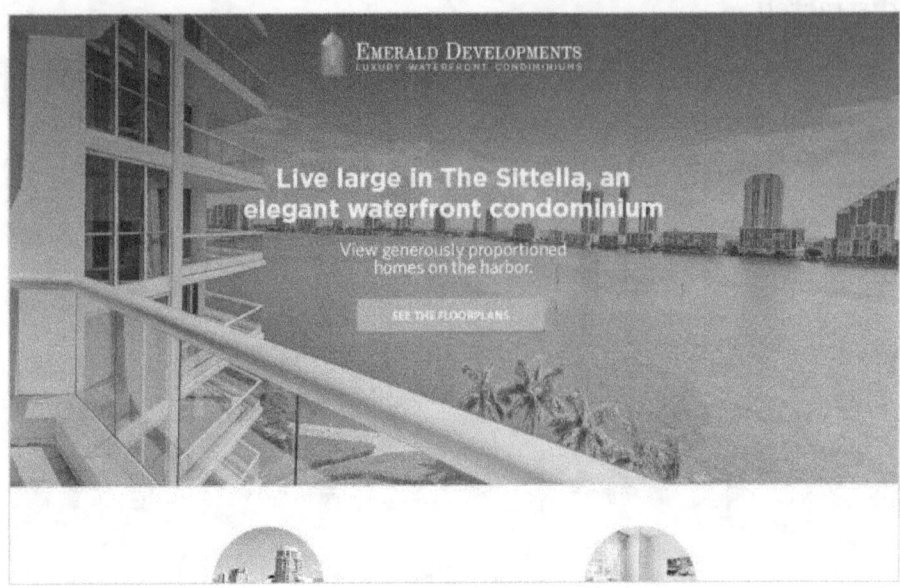

The following list outlines some of the marketing campaigns you might be running that will produce much better results when run with targeted landing pages:

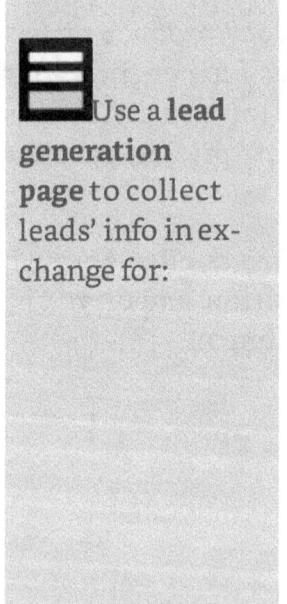 Use a **lead generation page** to collect leads' info in exchange for:

- Awesome whitepapers, ebooks, guides, reports, industry-specific checklists, and other content marketing or educational assets
- Subscription to your brand's newsletter, blogs, or other communication of interest to your target audience
- Registration to attend your in-person events, or to gain access to ecourses or webinars
- Requests for consultation services or access to recorded sessions (videos or slides)

Use a **click-through page** to prompt:

- An e-commerce purchase (direct visitors to a shopping cart)
- Registration for a free trial of your service
- Scheduling a demo or tour of your product

KEY TAKEAWAY Landing pages will improve your campaigns' conversion rates by providing your visitors with focused, relevant messaging and a clear, focused call to action. Remember that an individual landing page should only support a single campaign goal.

You should use a dedicated landing page for each and every marketing campaign you run.

WHAT KIND OF TRAFFIC TO SEND TO YOUR LANDING PAGES

Now that you know how landing pages will help you improve your marketing campaigns, you might be wondering how to get eyeballs on them.

Good question. While your main website should attract organic traffic and accommodate every type of visitor that ends up there – your **landing pages are built for *targeted*, campaign-specific traffic.**

You'll link to your dedicated landing pages each time that you:

- Direct traffic from promotional emails or an email campaign where you have a specific campaign goal like registering for a webinar, downloading an ebook, or scheduling a consultation
- Link to a page in campaign-specific social posts like a contest or event registration, and
- Run traffic through pay-per-click (PPC) ad campaigns which allows you to build focused, relevant pages and narrow your visitor's attention to a single call to action. PPC and Landing pages are like PB and J: made for each other. Because you can build a dedicated landing page for each of your ads and ad groups, landing pages will help you improve things like page relevance, time on page, and click-

through rates, which can massively improve your cost per click (and save you a ton of money!).

Chris Gold

The

5 elements of a high-converting landing page

Similar to a birthday cake which needs milk, eggs, flour, and water, a high converting landing page contains five important ingredients. These 5 elements are a recipe that give you a solid foundation for building a page that will inform and convert your visitors.

The most successful landing pages include:

1. Strong, contextual images including **a hero shot**
2. A selling **value proposition** in the form of **a headline and sub-headline**
3. A singular and focused **call to action**
4. Clearly outline **features and benefits** of your offer or service
5. **Social proof** or **testimonials** supporting your claims

Throughout the rest of this ecourse, you'll see these five elements come together to build the Emerald Developments landing page shown above, where the campaign goal is to generate leads by offering tours of a new waterfront condo development.

START WITH STRONG, CONTEXTUAL IMAGES

A big part of your job when building a landing page is to ensure it conveys quality and credibility. These two traits increase your chance of converting because they cater to your visitor's need to trust you before they buy into your call to action.

There are three types of images you'll typically use on your landing pages:

1. Hero Shot
2. Supporting Images
3. Icons

The **hero shot** is the main and most prominent image on your landing page. It should either convey to your visitors exactly what your page is about and what they'll get from it, or show your product or service in use.

Supporting images and **icons** should be high quality, on brand, and should communicate trust and credibility.

Here, Erin dives deeper into the role of images on your pages, and how to work with them in Unbounce:

KEY TAKEAWAY It should be clear from your hero shot *exactly* what your page is about. **Quick test:** If you removed all the words from your page, would your hero shot make complete sense?

Does it convey context?

Images are only the tip of the iceberg. They contribute to the feel of your page and show your product or service in action, but it's your page's copy that provides clarity and ultimately drives visitors toward your call to action.

YOUR HEADLINE AND SUB-HEADLINE

Copy is one of the most important parts of your landing page. Your headline is usually the first thing people notice when your page loads, so your copy needs to do some heavy lifting to tell your visitors they're in the right place, then keep them on the page.

As the first text that your visitor sees, great goals for the headline and sub-headline of your landing page, respectively, are to keep visitors from leaving your page, and to drive them forward to the rest of the page copy. Your headline and sub-headline should:

- Communicate the unique selling point of your page
- Have an obvious relationship to the ad or email that was clicked

By reading the headline and sub-headline of your page, the customer should be able to interpret what the page is about, and how it relates **directly** to the original ad or email that drove them there. This relationship from the original traffic source to your landing page is called message match.
Good Message Match

Bad Message Match

Broadly, here's how you'll add and edit text on your pages in Unbounce.

There are many more resources available to help you with writing page copy.

ADD YOUR CALL TO ACTION

Your call to action, whether it's a lead gen form or click-through button, is arguably the most critical element of your landing page. If there's no call to action, your visitors can't convert.

If your landing page copy does its job, your visitors should know exactly what to expect when they encounter your form, but there are some things you can do to ensure your form works like it should:

- Make sure that your lead gen form is prominent and that it's clear to prospects, why they should want to convert
- Include the minimum number of form fields needed to produce the highest quality conversion
- Customize your field labels for smoother integration with your 3rd party tools
- Use a button label that clearly states what will happen when users submit their info and completes the question "I want to..."
- Set up a Thank You page to optimize the post-click experience

Your CTA will is made all the more relevant by the supporting copy on your page that highlights the features and benefits of your offer. The next module covers how to build up benefits that convert.

SHARING THE (MOST IMPORTANT) BENEFITS OF YOUR OFFER

Your product benefits, results, and outcomes will be included in the body copy of your landing page.

When it comes to writing this type of content, the most common questions are about how to pick the most persuasive angle, and how *much* to write.

Copywriting expert Joanna Wiebe explains that to write the best body copy possible, you need to remember two foundational principles:

1. Customers' awareness dictates page length
   - The warmer your lead is, the less copy you need on your page, and vice versa.
2. Start with your conversion goal and work backwards
   - Make sure that the features and benefits you include are tied directly to the action you want your visitors to take.

Another essential use of copy is testimonials, or social proof, which we'll cover in the next module.

BRAG A BIT: A DASH OF SOCIAL PROOF

The last ingredient to add into the mix for a high-converting page is social proof – also known as customer testimonials.

Social proof is important because, even though you can *tell* people what your brand is all about, praise is always more believable when it comes from a secondary source. A good word from other brands or your loyal customers on your landing page acts as a stamp of approval and contributes to your credibility.

Here's an example of social proof in action on a landing page for Paper Anniversary. This brand sells traditional paper jewelry gifts and Anna, the founder, includes testimonials from the couples who made a purchase. The real photos of the couples enhance the social proof here, and ensure others reading the page that real customers love and recommend Anna's product.

KEY TAKEAWAY Social media buttons can go on your confirmation or thank you pages, but it's best to keep them off your landing pages as they distract folks away from your call to action. You don't want people sharing your page via Twitter, then getting caught up in the latest trending topic. You want them on your page converting!

Note that testimonials or social proof are only valuable insofar as they encourage your visitors to follow through with your call to action. They exist to:

- Ensure visitors they're making a wise choice choosing your brand over others
- Reinforce your great product or service, and
- Increase the desire people have for your offering

You also don't have to use quotations. With express permission you can display the logos of impressive companies who use your service on your landing page. Seeing that other brands use your service can be all the reassurance a new customer needs.

Overall, when done right, social proof can have a huge impact on your conversion rates.

KEY TAKEAWAY A testimonial is only good if it's authentic. Don't heavily edit your customers' words. Quotes should feel like they came from a person or they'll seem made up. Try asking open-ended questions to get the best quotes from your brand advocates.

And there you have it! You've added all five elements to your page. It's lookin' good and hopefully reads pretty persuasively at this point.

Watch the video below for a quick rundown of the Emerald Developments Real Estate example with all five elements in play:

KEY TAKEAWAY Although these are the five elements we recommend for a high-converting landing page, they're the base. The mold. The best-practice formula, we've found works pretty well. You can customize your pages however you like. There are no solid rules to conversion (as you'll find when you start A/B testing your pages to test your assumptions).

KEEP IMPROVING BY RUNNING AN A/B TEST

Throughout this course, you've learned where landing pages fit into your marketing campaigns, the 5 elements of a high converting page, and how to build landing pages in Unbounce.

But – here's the thing – the smartest marketers know that there's a way to continually get better and better results. In fact, your time to *really* shine as a marketer begins *after* you press the Publish button.

Not only do landing pages help you achieve better results by creating focused, targeted offers with great attention ratio and strong message match, they give you a way to isolate, test, and optimize each element on a page to achieve higher conversion rates on every campaign you run. Some might even say that testing is the best part about your newly created landing pages.

With a solid A/B test, you can do even more with less. Meaning you'll still run a campaign on the same marketing budget month to month, but you'll continually learn how to improve your conversion rates and results based on real data.

If, for example, you run a version A and version B of your page in which version A contains a video and version B does not, you'll be able to see which is the most persuasive for this particular audience, and this particular campaign.

No matter what combo of images, text, form fields, buttons, or social proof you add to your landing page, you should A/B test to determine what's working to convert and what's not.

MOVING FORWARD: IDEAS FOR ACTION

Now that you know how to use the Unbounce Page Builder, you're officially in business.
This is where things get good!

It's time to start running more effective campaigns with your newly acquired landing page savvy. If you weren't page-building in the app as you went along, here's a checklist to get you started.

Step 1: Choose a campaign to run.

4 Lead Gen Campaign Ideas (+the Landing Page Templates to Power Them)

Step 2: Build and publish your first landing page. Remember to include the following five elements:
1. A strong, contextual image (or 'Hero Shot')
2. The unique selling point (a headline and sub-headline)
3. Clearly writing benefit copy
4. Your call to action (the contact form and CTA button)
5. Social proof or testimonials

And

Step 3: Run your first A/B test to determine which elements of your page could use some improvement (Is your copy working to convert? How about testing out a new headline? Or better yet, different benefit blurb copy to speak to a different segment of your target market!)

The final quiz for this course will wrap things up and make sure you're ready to rock.

GET IN THE DRIVER'S SEAT

A good marketing strategy helps you create barriers to entry and produce wonderful, valuable content your clients can consume. You let them know how you can help them.

Now you're in the driver's seat. You are considering them as a possibility to become part of your community. They are also considering you but you're the one who set the system. You're the one who created the game. You're the one who caused this to happen in the first place.

Now, they made a decision through their own willpower, their own self-determinism.

If you do the same thing, you set up the game and the rules. If they're game with the rules, then they're in. The same goes if they're ready to be a part of the community based on how it operates and how it runs. If they're not, they're not.

The great thing about marketing strategies is you set up the game however you want to play it. You set up the game you think is best for everybody because you're the coach and the mentor. If they happen to like it, they can join. If they don't, it's cool. It's not a fit.

A marketing strategy also lets people know a small percentage of those we consider for this actually end up joining and are accepted into the community. It, therefore, becomes another way to source the right people.

Don't set up marketing strategies which let just anybody get on the phone with you. Set up ones that win big for everybody, a game you want to play, something that makes you want to spend your time and resources making it happen.

Don't forget you're the one who's reaching out to create this thing in the first place. Without you reaching out, nobody's going to find you. Set these marketing strategies in a way where they work for you: they fit your lifestyle, mission, vision, and dreams.

Hopefully, when you do it that way, you bring in dream clients who are aligned with your values and you are aligned with theirs. Together, that's what makes a great community.

Good Luck!

www.ingramcontent.com/pod-product-compliance
Lightning Source LLC
Chambersburg PA
CBHW070851220526
45466CB00005B/1953